TROPICAL FOREST MAMMALS

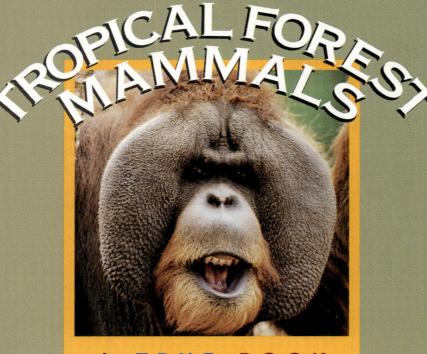

A TRUE BOOK

by

Elaine Landau

Children's Press®

A Division of Grolier Publishing

New York London Hong Kong Sydney
Danbury, Connecticut

For Michael—who has brought us more smiles than there are trees in a tropical forest.

Reading Consultant
Linda Cornwell
*Learning Resource Consultant
Indiana Department of Education*

Subject Consultant
Kathy Carlstead, Ph.D.
*National Zoological Park
Smithsonian Institution*

Orangutans swing through trees of the tropical forest.

Library of Congress Cataloging-in-Publication Data

Landau, Elaine.
        Tropical forest mammals / by Elaine Landau.
            p.   cm. — (A true book)
        Includes bibliographical references and index.
        Summary: Describes the physical characteristics and habits
of some rain forest mammals including the jaguar, tapir, orangutan,
sloth, and howler monkey.
        ISBN 0-516-20044-5 (lib. bdg.)   ISBN 0-516-26116-9 (pbk.)
        1. Rain forest animals—Tropics—Juvenile literature. 2. Mammals—
Juvenile literature. [1. Rain forest animals. 2. Mammals.] I. Title.
II. Series.
QLL112.L355   1996
599—dc20   96-3890
                                                                              CIP
                                                                               AC

Contents

Tropical Forests	5

Jaguars	13

Tapirs	19

Orangutans	25

Sloths	33

Howler Monkeys	39

To Find Out More	44

Important Words	46

Index	47

Meet the Author	48

Tropical forests are packed with life, but their future is uncertain.

Tropical Forests

The tropical forests of the world are lush green wonderlands. The trees there grow hundreds of feet high. Smaller trees and shrubs cover the ground. Thick rain forest vines wind around tree trunks and branches and hang like long ropes. Colorful orchids and other flowers add to the forest's beauty.

The tropical rain forest is one kind of tropical forest. This rich green area receives a huge amount of rainfall all year round. There are also seasonal tropical forests. These regions have a dry season as well as a wet season. Seasonal tropical forests do not have as many different kinds of trees and plants as rain forests do.

All tropical forests have a wide variety of animals,

Colors brighten the tropical forest.

however. Inch for inch, they contain more life than any other region on earth. Many tropical forest plants and animals cannot be found anywhere else.

This book looks at just a few of the many mammals that live in tropical forests. Mammals are animals with backbones and with larger brains than other types of animals. They are also the only animals that nurse their young. But some tropical forest mammals are at risk of becoming extinct. These animals often have been captured or killed by humans for various reasons. Many tropical forests animals have died after much of their natural habitat was destroyed.

In the past fifty years, more than 40 percent of the world's tropical forests have been destroyed for lumber or to make way for new towns and farms. Plans have been designed to save these rich woodlands. But in many parts of the world, tropical forests and the animals in them remain threatened.

NORTH AMERICA

Mexico

CENTRAL AMERICA

Jaguars are found in Mexico and in Central and South America.

SOUTH AMERICA

Howler monkeys are found in Central and South America.

Sloths are found in Central and South America.

E

A F

ANTA

N

W   E

S

OPE

ASIA

CA

Tapirs are found
in southeast Asia
and Central and
South America.

Sumatra

Borneo

AUSTRALIA

Orangutans
are found in
Sumatra and
Borneo.

TICA

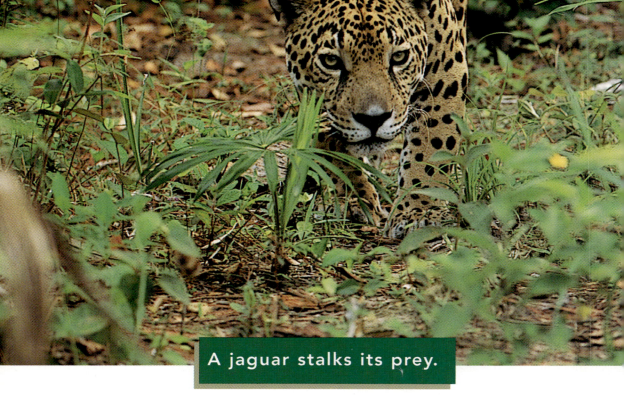

A jaguar stalks its prey.

Jaguars

Imagine walking through a forest knowing that a large wild cat is stalking you. Including its tail, the animal is 8.5 feet (2.6 meters) long and weighs about 300 pounds (136 kilograms). Out of the corner of your eye, you get a better look at it. Its coat is yellowish-beige with black spots and ringlike markings.

The animal is watching your every move. You are surprised because you know that this wild cat usually rests during the day. It is active after dark, when its deep, grunting call sounds through the forest. But now, at midday, it only makes low growling

Jaguars are fierce hunters of the forest.

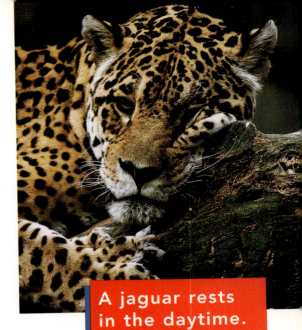

A jaguar rests in the daytime.

sounds as it gazes your way.

The animal on your trail is a fierce predator known as a jaguar. Sometimes it preys on monkeys, birds, turtles, and other small animals. But it is more likely to attack large animals, such as deer and tapirs. If its prey tries to escape the jaguar by jumping into a river or lake, it usually doesn't get far. The jaguar, an excellent swimmer, can easily overtake its prey in the water. The jaguar often uses its strength to move its kill from place to place. It can swim across a river with a deer in its mouth.

The number of jaguars in the world has declined because they have often been killed for their unique pelts.

But it is unlikely that you would become the jaguar's next meal. Jaguars rarely attack humans. These curious wild cats have been known to track people carefully without ever approaching them.

Jaguars have no enemies in their natural habitat. But through the years, humans have greatly reduced their numbers. Today, the jaguar is recognized as an endangered species and protected by law.

A Brazilian tapir

Tapirs

Tapirs are shy tropical forest dwellers. They weigh 500 to 700 pounds (227 to 318 kg) and stand about 3.5 feet (1.07 m) high at the shoulder.

Tapirs have an excellent sense of smell. They can thrust out their long snouts a full 12 inches (30 centimeters) to sniff plants they may want to eat. These animals feed on fruit, buds, leaves, and twigs of low-growing plants, trees, and shrubs. They also eat aquatic plants.

Although the tapir looks a lot like a large pig, it is actually related to the horse, zebra, and rhinoceros. The tapir doesn't look like any of these animals—but like the rhinoceros, it enjoys mud baths.

A tapir (above) finds a cool spot to rest. Tapirs (left) use their snouts to seek out food.

Tapirs are found in the swamps or marshy areas of tropical forests. They like to swim and are good divers. When fleeing from an enemy, they often jump into the water

Like all tapirs, this Malayan tapir spends a lot of time in the water.

to escape. Tapirs can remain underwater for a long time.

There are several species, or types, of tapirs. The Malayan tapir's front and limbs are dark brown or black, while the rest of its body is white. The tapirs of Central and South America are usually dark-brown or reddish.

In the wild, the tapir's main enemies are jaguars and tigers. Today, humans have caused the number of tapirs to decrease by destroying tropical forests.

A young tapir tries to reach some food.

Orangutan means "man of the woods."

Orangutans

Orangutans are humanlike in appearance. These great apes stand 4 to 5 feet (1.2 to 1.5 m) high and weigh about as much as a grown man.

An orangutan cannot be mistaken easily for a gorilla or chimpanzee. Sometimes jokingly called a "redhead,"

Orangutans look very different from their chimpanzee (above) and gorilla (right) relatives.

the orangutan has long, shaggy, reddish or orange hair. Only its face, feet, and hands are hairless, revealing the animal's dark brown skin.

The orangutan lives in trees and rarely comes down to the ground. Its body is well suited for this way of life. Its curved fingers grasp tree

Orangutans are known for their shaggy, red fur.

Living in the trees is easy when you have long arms like this orangutan.

branches easily, and its long arms are ideal for swinging through the forest.

Orangutans even sleep in trees. Every night the

orangutan builds a new nest out of broken branches and leaves. It usually abandons the nest the next morning and moves on to other trees. At times, an orangutan returns to the nest for a short nap during the day.

Most of the orangutan's waking hours are spent eating fruits and leaves. Unlike other great apes, these animals do not live in groups. A baby orangutan stays with its mother for the first three to four years of its life, however.

In the past, many zoos were willing to pay a great deal of money for a baby orangutan. Unfortunately, these babies could be obtained only by first killing their mothers. As orangutans only give birth about every four years, their numbers soon shrank.

Today, the orangutan is protected by local and international laws. The United

Baby orangutans stay close to their mothers.

States, along with other nations, prohibits bringing these animals into the country.

Sloths are unlike any other animal.

Sloths

If you saw a sloth in a tropical forest, you might think it was a strange-looking creature. These hairy animals have long limbs, rounded heads, peglike teeth, and narrow curved feet with strong claws. Sloths are nearly tailless, and their ears are barely noticeable.

These slow-moving animals spend much of their lives hanging upside down in trees. They eat and sleep that way. A sloth's body may remain hanging from a tree branch even after the animal dies.

Sloths often hang upside-down

Sloths do not leave the trees, even to sleep.

Sloths seldom come down from the trees. They eat leaves, buds, and twigs there. And a sloth can easily hide from its predators in a tree. The animal's long, thick brownish-gray hair often becomes covered with bright green algae. Predators passing by think the animal is part of the tree.

There are two types of sloths—the two-toed sloth and the three-toed sloth. The two-toed sloth, also known as the unau, is about 2 feet (0.6 m) long. It has two toes on each of its front feet. The three-toed sloth, called the ai, is slightly smaller than a two-toed sloth. It has three toes on its front feet.

Green algae on this sloth's fur helps it blend in to the trees (above); a hungry sloth (right).

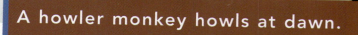

A howler monkey howls at dawn.

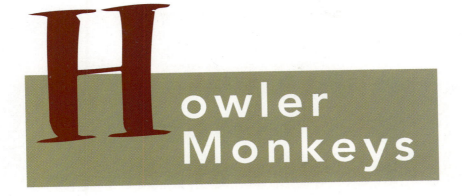Howler Monkeys

Can you guess from its name what the howler monkey is best known for? If you said the howling sound it makes, you are right. Just as roosters crow at daybreak, howler monkeys give out a very loud roar at dawn.

Despite its loud howl, the howler monkey is not very

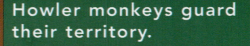

Howler monkeys guard their territory.

large. Usually these animals are only 2 feet (0.6 m) long and weigh up to 20 pounds (9 kg). Howler monkeys have strong tails, however, that are about as long as their bodies. Howlers have black, brown, or reddish fur, depending on their species. But their hairless faces are always black.

These monkeys live in groups of about twenty animals with many more females than males. Each group has its own territory, which it carefully guards. These monkeys howl

Female black howler monkeys and a newborn

in the early morning to let other groups know their location—and to warn them to stay away. A howler monkey group will also roar if another group comes too close to its boundaries.

Howler monkeys sleep in the trees. They also eat there, feed-

A red howler monkey feeds on leaves.

ing on leaves, buds, and fruits. Howlers especially like figs.

Full-grown howlers have few predators in the wild. Yet, like so many other tropical forest animals, their numbers have declined in recent years because of the destruction of their habitats by humans.

To Find Out More

Here are more places to learn about tropical forest mammals:

Books

Arnold, Caroline. **Orangutan.** Morrow Junior Books, 1990.

Brooks, Bruce. **Predator!** Farrar Straus and Giroux, 1991.

Gibbons, Gail. **Nature's Green Umbrella.** Morrow Junior Books, 1994.

Greenaway, Theresa. **Jungle.** Knopf, 1994.

Lemmon, Tess. **Apes.** Ticknor & Fields, 1993.

Ryden, Hope. **Your Cat's Wild Cousins.** Lodestar, 1991.

Yolen, Jane. **Welcome to the Greenhouse.** G.P. Putnam, 1993.

Simon, Seymour. **Big Cats.** HarperCollins, 1991.

Organizations

American Zoo and Aquarium Association
7979-D Old Georgetown Rd.
Bethesda, MD 20814
(301) 907-7777
http://www.aza.org/

Earth Island Institute
300 Broadway, Suite 28
San Francisco, CA 94133-3312
(415) 788-3666
http://www.earthisland.org/ei/strp/strpca.html

Zoological Society of San Diego
P.O. Box 271
San Diego, CA 92112-0271
http://www.sandiegozoo. org/

The Amazon Trail. MECC's Trail Series.
A CD-ROM filled with problem-solving, navigational skills, and reading, focused on South American history and the ecosystem. Ages 8+

The Rainforest. ZooGuide's Library.
Explore the amazing world of the rain forest through animation, photos, and video on this CD-ROM. Ages 8+

The Bigger Big Cats Info Page
http://sys3.cs.usu.edu/ faculty/cannons/cats.html
Meet jaguars, tigers, lions, and more!

Animals of Brazil
http://www.demon.co. uk/ltamaraty/fauna.html
Learn all about the birds, reptiles, and mammals of the world's largest tropical country.

Costa Rica Handbook
http://www-swiss.ai. mit.edu/cr/moon/ mammals.html
Discover lots of information about monkeys, jaguars, sloths, and tapirs.

Rainforest Action Network
http://www.ran.org/ran/ kids_action/index.html
The Kids' Action Page has great stuff on the rain forests!

Important Words

algae a type of green plant that lives in wet or moist environments

aquatic living or growing in water

endangered at risk of dying out

extinct no longer existing

habitat an animal's environment

pelt the furry skin of an animal

predator an animal that lives by hunting other animals

prey an animal hunted by another for food

shrub a thick low-growing bush

species a particular type of animal

stalk to hunt or track down

Index

(**Boldface** page numbers
  indicate illustrations.)

algae, 36, **37**
chimpanzees, 25, **26**
endangered species, 17
food, 15, 20, **21**, **23**, 29,
  35, 42–43, **42**
fur, 13–14, **16**, 25–26, **27**,
  35, **37**, 40
gorillas, 25, **26**
hair. See fur
howler monkeys, **10**, **38**,
  39–43, **40**, **41**, **42**, **43**
humans, 9, 17, 23, 25,
  43, **43**
hunting, **14**, 15–16, **16**
jaguars, **10**, **12**, 13–17,
  14, **15**, **16**, 23
laws, 17, 30–31
Malayan tapir, 22, **22**
mammals, 7–8

orangutans, **2**, **11**, **24**,
  25–31, **27**, **28**, **31**
predators, 15, 21, 23,
  35, 36, 43
seasonal tropical forests, 6
shelter, 29
sloths, **10**, **32**, 33–36, **34**,
  35, **37**
smell, 19
tails, 40
tapirs, **11**, 15, **18**, 19–23,
  21, **22**, **23**
territory, **40**, 41–42
three-toed sloth, 36
tigers, 23
tropical forests, **4**, 5–9,
  7, **8**
tropical rain forest, 6
two-toed sloth, 36
United States, 30–31
young, 8, **23**, 29–30, **31**, **41**
zoos, 30

Meet the Author

Elaine Landau worked as a newspaper reporter, children's book editor, and youth services librarian before becoming a full-time writer. She has written more than ninety books for young people.

Ms. Landau finds the vast range of animal and plant life in tropical forests overwhelmingly wonderful. Her favorite tropical forest animals is the orangutan, while the orchid is the tropical forest flower she likes best.